THE HERALD WIND

THE HERALD WIND
TRANSLATIONS OF SUNG DYNASTY POEMS, LYRICS AND SONGS

By CLARA M. CANDLIN

WITH AN INTRODUCTION BY
L. CRANMER-BYNG

FOREWORD BY
DR. HU SHIH

GREENWOOD PRESS, PUBLISHERS
WESTPORT, CONNECTICUT

Library of Congress Cataloging in Publication Data

Main entry under title:

The Herald wind.

    Reprint. Originally published: London : J. Murray, 1955.
    1. Chinese poetry--Translations into English.
2. English poetry--Translations from Chinese.
I. Candlin, Clara M. (Margaret), 1883-   .
PL2658.E3H4   1981   895.1'14'08   81-2621
ISBN 0-313-23079-X (lib. bdg.)   AACR2

This is a reprint of the 1955 reprint edition. First edition printed in 1933.

Reprinted with the permission of John Murray Publishers, Ltd.

Reprinted from an original copy in the collections of Tompkins Cortland Community College, Learning Resources Center.

Reprinted in 1981 by Greenwood Press
A division of Congressional Information Service, Inc.
88 Post Road West, Westport, Connecticut 06881

Printed in the United States of America

10 9 8 7 6 5 4 3 2 1

To

MY FATHER

WHOSE FOOTSTEPS I DID
NOT FOLLOW, UNTIL HE
HAD VANISHED

Yet these people (the Chinese) also are richly endowed with that mysterious creative power of imagination which gives to genius its light and to love its glory. . . .

It has lifted them, as it has lifted us, above the dust, has made them fellow-inheritors of the gifts of time, and taught them to build out of the rude and sordid conditions of their actual life an ideal world, wide and spacious, and filled with forms of nobleness and beauty.

The REV. GEORGE T. CANDLIN in *Chinese Fiction.*

ACKNOWLEDGMENT

My thanks are due to Mr. H. L. Chow for reading the lyrics to me and for his decisive criticism over the interpretations. To Dorothy Rutherfurd, Dr. Mary Ramsay, and C. K. Millar for their unfailing encouragement, without which the translations would never have been achieved. Several of these poems have appeared in *The Poetry Review*, and I am further indebted to the Editor for his kind introduction to the Editor of this Series.

C. M. C.

EDITORIAL NOTE

THE object of the editor of this series is a very definite one. He desires above all things that, in their humble way, these books shall be the ambassadors of good-will and understanding between East and West, the old world of Thought, and the new of Action. He is confident that a deeper knowledge of the great ideals and lofty philosophy of Oriental thought may help to a revival of that true spirit of Charity which neither despises nor fears the nations of another creed and colour.

J. L. CRANMER-BYNG.

50, Albemarle Street,
London, W. 1.

CONTENTS

	PAGE
INTRODUCTION	13
FOREWORD	27

WÊN T'ING-CHUN:
    Fading in Spring 31

WEI CHUANG:
    The Dream 32
    The South 33

LI LÜ:
    The Wanderer's Woe 34
    The Emperor's Lament—I . . . 35
    The Emperor's Lament—II . . . 35
    My Southern Kingdom 36

YEN SHU:
    From a Height 38
    The Listless Beauty 39

OU-YANG HSIU:
    At the New Year Lantern Festival . . 40
    When You are Gone 40
    To the Dancing Girl on North Lake . 41

CHANG HSIEN:
    At the Feast 43
    The Plums hear the Music of her Flute . 44

YEN CHI-TAO:
    Let the Harp Speak 45

CONTENTS

	PAGE
LIU YUNG:	
The Butterfly Loves the Flowers	46
I Daily Look for You	47
SSŬ-MA KUANG:	
The Tryst	49
WANG AN-SHIH:	
Spring Night	50
Under Thatched Eaves	50
Late in the Tower Sitting Idly	51
LEI CHÊN:	
Village Evenings	52
SU SHIH:	
The Waiting Statesman	53
Wygelia	54
Su Chieh	54
CH'ÊNG HAO:	
The Autumn Months	56
Spring Days Come Suddenly	57
CH'IN KUAN:	
Of Fading Blossoms	58
With the Day	59
Fickle Youth	59
HUANG T'ING-CHIEN:	
Spring	61
Spring's Return	61
Divining	62
Too Late	63
CHOU PANG-YEN:	
After Carousing	64
A Wind-Tossed Cloud	65
I Write to Her	65
She Sings the Song of Golden Threads	66

CONTENTS

	PAGE
LI C'HING-CHAO (*Poetess*):	
The Widow	68
The Widow	69
HSIANG HAO:	
At Early Dawn	70
CHU TUN-JU:	
The Peerless Lady	71
The Fisherman	72
By the Brook	74
CHU HSI:	
Parable of Learning Truth	75
Pomegranate Flowers in Spring	75
HSIN CH'I-CHI:	
On the Road	76
Life	77
Sorrow's Taste	78
On the Road to Po-Shan	78
My New House on Lake Tai	79
Midnight Among the Hills	80
At Midnight I Hear the Monastery Bell	81
She is Gone	82
The Tune of the Stream	82
YEH SHIH:	
The Little Garden	83
LU YU:	
The Warriors	84
The Aged Warrior	85
To-morrow Everything Will Change	85
The Pilgrim Thinks and Dreams	86
Late in the Year	87
The Melancholy Voice of the Owl	88

CONTENTS

	PAGE
CHIANG K'UEI:	
White Plum Blossoms	89
The Lantern Festival	90
LIU K'Ê-CHUANG:	
To a Dancing Girl	93
A Dream	94
Flowers	95
The Oriole Shuttle	96
CHIANG CHIEH:	
Time is Leaving us Behind	97
Autumn Sounds	98
Who Comes to Gather Flowers?	99
MISCELLANEOUS LYRICS AND SONGS:	
In Mid-Autumn	101
Pan Ch'iao's Philosophy	102
My Beautiful One	103
Spring Tidings	104
Thoughts of Love	105
Mêng Chiang Nü	108
Ch'ing Ming	110
To Mongolia	112

INTRODUCTION

THE years between A.D. 906 and 1278 are by far the most important in the history of Chinese art and culture. For this period alone has witnessed the full fruition of the Chinese spirit, and the dynasties that follow the Sung are those of China's decadence. They have their brief intervals of renewal under the native Ming and the great Manchu Emperors K'ang Hsi and Ch'ien Lung, but these are summer's last challenge to winter, her few halcyon days of brief triumph and passing glamour that return in October and November. And there is this to bear in mind above all—that the history of the Chinese spirit, in religion, philosophy, and art, is the history of a single tradition with eventful periods of reinterpretation. Nothing is ever superimposed from without as in the case of Europe with its eastern religion and Greek culture. Every brand of Tartar, of Mongol, or Manchu conqueror has imposed its temporary will upon the surface of this great and ancient civilization and achieved nothing but ultimate effacement and absorption into the

Chinese matrix. In this denial of any alien influence upon the national spirit an exception appears to be called for in favour of Indian Buddhism. But the exception dissolves in the light of modern criticism which has amply proved that so far from Indian Buddhism dominating Chinese thought it was Chinese thought that profoundly modified the former. The Ch'an Hüe school of Buddhism, better known to us under its Japanese name of Zen, was founded by Bodhidharma in the sixth century. Henceforth it becomes impossible to form any estimate of Chinese art or literature without possessing some knowledge of a school of thought in which the foremost poets and artists of the day graduated. For Zen, beginning with "illumination through self-concentration," emerges with the Sung dynasty from a purely passive philosophy into one of identification of thought with action. It sheds its Indian shell and becomes responsive to the Chinese world of energy. The creative glow follows the visionary light and art is born, as self-illumination passes into self-fusion with the objects thus revealed around it. This is the very essence of Zen teaching contained in the Japanese word *Yugen* which stands for *identification* and is itself based on the recognition of the community of life with life. A story told of Li Lung Mien, the greatest of all the Sung painters, amusingly illustrates this point. In early life he was passionately fond of painting horses and spent hours gazing at those in the Imperial stables.

At length a Buddhist priest reproved him, saying, "The disposition of all living creatures is determined by influences gathered upon them during past æons by time. Now your mind is taken up solely by horses. Take care lest by process of metempsychosis you become yourself a horse."[1]

From a cultural point of view the Sung dynasty is but a prolongation of the T'ang. A stormy interval of fifty-five years intervenes, a time of mushroom dynasties and little local Courts where, notably among the Southern T'angs, the great T'ang tradition was fostered and preserved. And, moreover, the lapse of the central control encouraged the spirit of individualism, of divine difference as opposed to drab uniformity. So when T'ai Tsu, the founder of the Sung dynasty, ascended the throne he inherited nearly the whole of the T'ang tradition of wisdom and beauty with something added and something lost. The T'ang spirit still flowed along river and canal of the new Capital of Kai-feng-fu in the province of Honan but with a subtle change. In what way shall we discriminate between the old and the new forces so apparently intermingled ? In the first place a fresh impetus is now beginning to make itself felt throughout the Empire. Book-printing

[1] *An Introduction to the History of Chinese Pictorial Art*, by Herbert Giles, p. 124.

16   INTRODUCTION

known under the T'angs was only adapted for general use through the foresight of a certain evergreen Chinese Vicar of Bray, Fêng Tao (881–954), so that its full influence was only felt in the years that followed, when the stone slab gave place to the wooden printing block and literature was disseminated in all the provinces of China. "It was then," says Richard Wilhelm in his *History of Chinese Civilization*, "that those works were created which have furnished a pattern for all time as regards printing technique, lay-out, and an harmonious and artistic appearance." And there are other influences started in the T'ang which now begin to assert themselves in the later period. The favourite symbol of Taoist philosophy is that of water; and Taoist fluidity permeated all the ideas of the earlier age. And when the two contending forces of Taoism and Confucianism were equally balanced the great balanced spirit of China revealed itself in all its rich humanity and artistic splendour. The Taoist lost his aloofness from the affairs of men and the Confucianist his aloofness from the latent spirit of God in Nature, the Divine Collaborator of Man in the Universe. For generations Confucianism had prevailed through its control of the educational system. Now the study circles (*shu-yüan*) of the new spirit began to appear.

They had arisen [says Wilhelm] in opposition to the official system of examinations, which was becoming more frigid and formal, and was useful only as the gateway to an official career. Their aim was intimacy, warmth of feeling, sincere conviction; education was to be promoted for the sake of its ennobling effect on character, not as a mere stepping-stone to a political career.

In these days when careers of every kind are being overshadowed by politics it is interesting to note a distinct tendency on the part of the British Broadcasting Corporation to promote study-circles of similar ideals to the *shu-yüan* of the Sung. For the most part, as Wilhelm points out, these schools were " hidden away in wooded valleys or along the shores of rivers, in some idyllic spot. There the master dwelt with his disciples, and knowledge and education were imparted by direct personal tuition." This is a matter of paramount importance in any study of the influences at work moulding the rising generations of Sung statesmen, artists and philosophers. And it must be pointed out that the three great religions of China, Confucianism, Taoism and Buddhism, all played their allotted parts therein. The *shu-yüan* were in direct accord with the Confucian ideal, since the Master himself gathered around him a school of this nature in his old age. They were also in keeping with the Taoist worship of beauty both visible and invisible in the secret life of things, and the Buddhist sense of profound reverence and dedication to the ultimate reality and attainment of Buddhahood: "No Church was this, but a community of mutually sympathetic souls in which doctrinal differences, even antagonisms, could exist without destroying its *esprit de corps*." The genius of Richard Wilhelm has given us in a sentence a vision into the past of China's golden age which is also an outlook into our own future when we shall have laid down not merely our weapons of physical warfare but the armour of our impenetrable spiritual, and intellectual, and national pride.

As the Sung era unfolds we note both rise and fall, growth and decay, in the various arts as compared with their previous state under the T'angs. The art of sculpture is beginning to decay swiftly, while that of poetry is slowly receding from its high level. Painting on the other hand soars to heights which can only be compared with those attained by the Italian Renaissance. And the great art of the Chinese potters reaches its full zenith with the porcelains of Ting Chou of the Northern Sung and those of Ch'ing te Chen of the Southern dynasty. For it was the destiny of the Sung line to be broken by its enemies the Nü-chên or Golden Tartars and suffer the loss of its northern capital Kai-feng-fu in A.D. 1127 when Hui Tsung, the greatest artist of his day and the most abject Emperor, set out for his ultimate destination, a nameless grave on the

INTRODUCTION

Sungari River in the far north-east, a pilgrimage of pain which lasted eight years. His ninth son Prince K'ang, who had escaped to Nanking, assumed the throne under the title of Kao Tsung and in 1138 transferred the capital to Hangchow.

The new capital of the Southern Sung takes up and continues the tradition of Kai-feng-fu in the north. Yet something is added through the mellowing charm of the climate, the presence of the surrounding hills and the reflecting mirror of Lake Hsi Hu. Not the literary class alone but the whole nation worshipped at the shrine of natural beauty. At sunset artist and artisan were one in the tribute they paid to the haunting spirit of peace that hovered above the jewelled waters. And the hour of dusk was also the hour of pilgrimage to the hill-shrines of Buddhism where personality was laid aside and man entered into communion with the Universal Source of Life. The Chinese Zen priests were no mere contemplatives or performers of ceremonial rites. There is a long and illustrious line of artist-priests in the Sung period who did not confine themselves to purely religious subjects beginning with Chu Jan (*circa* A.D. 975) and Yuan Ai, and continuing with Mu Ch'i, who flourished towards the end of the Southern Sung, and his disciple, Mu An. The importance of Mu Ch'i cannot be over-estimated, for, as Fenellosa has pointed out : " All the great Japanese artists, including Sesshu and Noami, have built upon him. Kano Motonobu, in his softer style, grows out of him. The whole Kinkakuji school of Kioto follows him." What is behind this Sung worship of landscape and the individual treatment of life in flower and tree ?

In the *Guide to an Exhibition of Chinese and Japanese Paintings* at the British Museum Mr. Laurence Binyon has given the answer:

> Man is not conceived of as detached from, or opposed to, external nature ; rather there is the thought of one life or soul manifested in both, so that the springing and withering of the wayside grasses are felt to be something really related to the life of the human spirit contemplating them, and the apparition of beauty in fresh snow, or rising moon, or blossoms opening on bare spring branches, seems the manifestation of a life and a power in which men also share.

It is this feeling of being at home in the Universe and akin with life in all its manifestations, " this note of joyous liberation " which is the very wellspring of all Sung inspiration both in art and literature. If you will listen to Ssu-k'ung T'u, most philosophic of the later T'ang poets, you will find it expressed in a twelve-line poem that yet conveys a deep sincerity and intimate spiritual experience. It is called " Close Woven."

> In all things there are veritable atoms,
> Though the senses cannot perceive them,
> Struggling to emerge into shape
> From the wondrous workmanship of God.

INTRODUCTION

> Water flowing, flowers budding,
> The limpid dew evaporating,
> An important road, stretching far,
> A dark path where progress is slow. . . .
> So words should not shock,
> Nor thought be inept.
> But be like the green of Spring,
> Like snow beneath the moon.

Professor Giles who translates it, in his *History of Chinese Literature*, adds this significant footnote to the last line : " Each invisible atom of which combines to produce a perfect whole." Though, as I have already pointed out, poetry is beginning to decline from its zenith, reached in the eighth century when Tu Fu, Li Po, Ch'ang Ch'ien and most of the famous T'ang poets flourished, the Sung age has made its own distinct contribution of great poetry. The foremost place has been assigned by common consent to Ou-yang Hsiu whose *Autumn Dirge* is a masterpiece of solemn beauty and grave thought. The claim of Su Shih, better known as Su Tung-p'o, has been disputed by critics and ardently affirmed by others like Mr. Drummond le Gros Clark whose recent *Selections from the Works of Su Tung-p'o* have done much to re-establish his reputation.[1] Nor is it possible to exclude Lu Yu of the Southern Sungs, the soldier-poet who, as Mrs. Grantham reminds us,

[1] Published by Jonathan Cape, 1931.

on his deathbed exhorted his son to send him the good news, if ever it should come true:

> When at last Imperial armies march
> To reconquer the Central Plain,
> Forget not at your household worship
> To whisper to your father's soul.[1]

It is the last flash of the indomitable Chinese spirit against the Tartar night that overwhelms it and after Lu Yu the great tradition is broken. All the poems here translated belong to the lyric order of short poems as distinguished from the descriptive prose-poems or *Fu*. Mostly they are wayside shrines raised by travellers to hallow the memory of some hour of contemplation and community. They are word pictures never elaborated but sketched swiftly with here and there a suggestion of colour and a frugality of line whose only comparison is that of the later Greek idylls. They are often, though not always, impersonal, and this is especially the case with poets of Taoist and Buddhist leanings. You can almost distinguish the Confucians among them through this intrusion of personality. And yet, even so, there is restraint—the restraint of the Chinese spirit that prefers to suggest, to indicate, and bow you on your way. For the outlook on this world of changing phenomena is essentially religious and reverential, questing the spirit that underlies each passing form and the unity between

[1] *Hills of Blue*, by A. E. Grantham, p. 362.

man and nature. Therefore to the Chinese artist you are no tourist but, like him, a pilgrim on the divine adventure. And the pilgrim must be welcomed with all courtesy, but in the end he must find his way alone.

Chinese poetry is often tinged with the sadness of evanescence. This is apparent from the very beginning in the ancient songs and ballads, so different, where the poet speaks of himself, from the gracious and grateful hymns of the Vedic Rishis with their clear optimism and response to the kindly deities that ruled beyond the Indus. Only the Taoists like Chang Chih-ho and Ssu k'ung T'u escape its influence since they have identified themselves with the secret and abiding beauty of the world, and to them—

> Since life and death in cycles come and go,
> Of little moment are the days to spare.

Yet there is nothing of despair or pessimism in this artist's recognition of the truth that visible beauty is enhanced by its impermanence and more desirable from the knowledge that even as we stretch out our hand—

> It eludes us and is gone.

With the rise of the Sung another note is heard for the first time. Mrs. Grantham in *Hills of Blue* points out that—

Tragedy was the new thing that broke upon the vision of the Sung artists with all the force of an unexpected dawn. . . .

It was the Sung masters who first visualized the poignant grief hidden in the heart of creative joy. And they pictured it in mountain summits desolate amid wild storms, in pines wind-twisted and smitten with old age that must surely turn to death, in mists dissolving into nothingness, in man gazing out into infinitude whose vastness dooms his loftiest aspirations to halt for ever before the unattainable.

And this is man's own tragedy of which the wind-twisted pine overhanging the abyss becomes the symbol. It is depicted on the silken rolls of Li Lung Mien, of the Buddhist priest Mu Ch'i and his followers, and you may hear it in many of the descriptive prose poems, above all in the magnificent *Autumn Dirge* of Ou-yang Hsiu—

> Stay! there yet is man—
> Man the divinest of all things, whose heart
> Has known the shipwreck of a thousand hopes,
> Who bears a hundred wrinkled tragedies
> Upon the parchment of his brow, whose soul
> Strange cares have lined and interlined until
> Beneath the burden of life his inmost self
> Bows down. And swifter still he seeks decay
> When groping for the unattainable
> Or grieving over continents unknown.

But in the end " Nature is greater than the grief of gods " or mortals, and in the long struggle between the mountain spirit and the fevered stress of the human hive beneath it is the mountain that prevails. Long ago the Chinese poet had realized what the West is beginning dimly to perceive, that—

Truth lay, not in rebellion, not in abnegation, *but in a passionate acceptance of necessity*. And in the light of such a vision life became worth living; not for any statable purpose, but purely for the sake of being alive. Joy was its own justification, endeavour its own goal.[1]

L. CRANMER-BYNG.

[1] *Korea of the Japanese*, by H. B. Drake.

FOREWORD

ABOUT sixty of the poems in this collection are specimens of the *tz'u*. The *tz'u* is a song written to musical melody. It began as popular songs of unknown authorship sung by the public entertainers and dancers. Occasionally, some poet who was attracted by the melody of these popular airs, would compose a new song to the music played by his favourite lady. From A.D. 800 on, the popularity and freedom of this new type of song-making began to attract the attention of an increasing number of poets and the *tz'u* soon became a fashion in the world of letters.

The *tz'u* differs from the older forms of poetry (*shih*) in several aspects. First, whereas the older poems were usually written in regular lines of either five or seven syllables each, the *tz'u* are usually irregular in the length of the lines, varying from one syllable to nine or eleven. This variation makes the lines better suited to the natural pauses of speech.

Secondly, though irregular in the lines, every *tz'u* is a song composed to a definite tune, and is therefore necessarily limited by the pattern of the melody. There were thousands of tunes, but all the songs written to a particular tune must conform to its particular pattern.

Thirdly, the *tz'u* is essentially lyric in nature and very brief in form, and is, therefore, incapable of expressing big themes of epic narration or didactic meditation. Practically no *tz'u* is of more than two stanzas each, and few of the tunes have over one hundred words or syllables. Some poets of the Sung dynasty tried to use this new poetic form for purposes other than lyrical; and a few of them actually succeeded in producing some well-known didactic poems in the strict form of *tz'u*. But in general the *tz'u* is only suited to small sentiments of love and concise passing reflections of life. The great poets of the age, like Su Shih and Lu Yu, who were all masters of the *tz'u*, continued to produce their great poems in the older forms of *shih* which, though regular in the length of each line, are unlimited in the number of lines and stanzas.

After the twelfth century, the *tz'u* developed into the *ch'u-tsŭ*, which were also songs written to popular airs, but which had even greater irregularity in the length of the lines and more freedom in versification. As these songs, the *tz'u* and the freer *ch'u-tsŭ*, were too limited in form to be useful media for historical and dramatical recitals, the ingenious reciters hit upon the idea of combining several of the popular tunes into series or serial melodies to which they sang their historical and epic narratives. When the stories were told in the third person we had the epic; and when the narration took the form of direct dialogues between the characters in the stories, it could be acted on the stage and we had the drama. All the singing parts of the dramas of the Yuan and Ming dynasties were written to existing popular tunes and were therefore historically derived from the *tz'u*.

HU SHIH.

WÊN T'ING-CHUN

A.D. 850–?

A NATIVE of Shan Hsi, an official and poet, whose works are mostly lost. He opens the door for the Sung poets. One book of miscellaneous essays and poems is in existence. It is called *Collected Flowers*.

FADING IN THE SPRING

A knot of hair
Lies low
Upon her neck;
Her long
And narrow eyebrows each
Are painted skilfully;
Yet are her thoughts
All day
Astray.
Because of you
She thinner grows,
In this,
The season of a hundred kinds
Of flowers.

WEI CHUANG

A.D. 855–920

A RENOWNED poet of the declining years of the T'ang dynasty who wrote a long poem of a great battle that took place in those days of confusion. He was a leader in the reorganization under the Sungs and dictated many of the new laws.

THE DREAM

Dreaming at midnight,
Last night I saw you and talked with you long.
As in the old days, your cheeks were like peach bloom;
Eyes often downcast and eyebrows like willow leaves;
Half the time happy and half the time bashful,
Willing to leave me yet lingering near.
Then I awakened.
Sadly I found it a dream.

THE SOUTH

All men speak
Well of the South.
Travellers all
Stay in the South,
Till they're aged.
Lakes and streams
Vie in blueness
With the sky.
In the gay
Painted barges
Raindrops make
Music for you
As you sleep.
One there is,
Like a fairy,
By the wine-stove.
Frozen snow
Are her wrists.
Travellers say
" Till old age
Stay in the South."
Stay in the South
While you're young
Or you'll be
Broken hearted.

LI YÜ

A.D. 961-973

Li Yü was the last of the Southern T'ang Emperors, who became a fugitive when his dynasty was overthrown by the Sungs. His poetry is full of sad recollections. It was reported that he was finally poisoned by the will of the Sung Emperor, on the 7th of the 7th moon at the age of 42.

THE WANDERER'S WOE

Alone, and silently,
I climb
The West pavilion tower.
The moon is like a curving hook;
And in the still Catalpa Court
Is crystal autumn locked.

Unsevered
Though sundered.
In chaos, yet
In order set.
This strange commotion in the heart
Is but the wanderer's woe.

THE EMPEROR'S LAMENT

Faded are the woodland flowers of spring,
All too soon, too soon.
Chilly rain unbidden comes at dawn :
Late at night the wind.

Guttering candles :
Friendly revelries :
When will days like these return again ?
Life is ever fraught with woe :
Rivers ever eastward flow.

THE EMPEROR'S LAMENT

The fair spring flowers,
The autumn moons,
When will they cease to be ?
The vanished past,
How much of it
Is wrapped in memory ?
Last night the East wind shook
My roof again ;
And I,
Beneath the moon,
Recalled
My hapless kingdom in the South.
The graven parapet,
The terrace of pale jade
Should still be there ;

But all the carmine cheeks
Are changed.
You ask,
How much of sorrow is there left
Within my heart?
And I reply
A spring-tide river full
Of water, flowing East.

MY SOUTHERN KINGDOM

Without my window screen
The rain is falling;
And listless is the spirit of the Spring.
My silken quilt is light,
Nor can it ward me from the cold
Of early dawn.
This alien life
I know not in my dreams.
There pleasures ever lure me on.

Yet never must I lean, alone,
Upon the balcony
And let my spirit fly
Across that boundless plain.
How easy then to part!
How hard to venture back!

Flow on, deep streams.
Fade, flowers, and fall.

The Spring is past.
'Tis Heaven, when Spring is here;
But days are only common days
When Spring is gone.

YEN SHU

A.D. 1042

A GIFTED poet who wrote essays at the age of seven. Greatly praised by Sung historians. He influenced the poetry of the Sung dynasty.

FROM A HEIGHT

Mimosa flowers,
And gold chrysanthemums
In fragrance riot in the autumn sun.
The distant village, like a picture, glows
With intermingled red
And yellow trees.

The streams flow shallowly,
The azure sky is far;
And from this height
The eye discerns no end
To roads unlimited.
When wild geese pass,
The thoughts fly boundlessly.

THE LISTLESS BEAUTY

When catkins bloom
The Spring wind blows.
How can they bear to part?
With silken draperies
She screens her tears,
And lets the stains
Of powder mar her robe.
How can they bear to part?
A thousand times:
Ten thousand times
She tries
To keep him yet she fails.

With wine in cups
Of jade:
With sorrow's furrowed brow;
The empty, sundered heart
Is like a kite
With severed string.
She knows not where
They afterwards may meet
On earth.
Perhaps in dreams
She often, often will
Fly back
To him.

OU-YANG HSIU

A.D. 1017–1072

A Sung dynasty statesman, poet, and historian of great fame, whose tablet is to be found in the Confucian temple.

AT THE NEW YEAR LANTERN FESTIVAL

Last year the first month's moon was full.
Like day the flower-fair lanterns shone.
The moon climbed to the willow tops.
I trysted her at yellow dusk.

This year the first month's moon is full.
The moon and lanterns are the same.
I cannot see her anywhere.
My Spring robe sleeves are wet with tears.

WHEN YOU ARE GONE

When you are gone,
I know not whether you
Are near or far;

And all that meets my eyes
Cold melancholy brings.
You gradually go,
Are gradually distant and epistles cease.
As waters vast
Where sink the little fish.
Where shall I go
To ask of you?

'Tis late
The wind raps out
An autumn tune,
Among the bamboo trees.
Ten thousand leaves :
A thousand sounds
And all are sorrowful.
I seek for you in dreams ;
Reclining on my lonely pillow ; yet
My dreams have no avail ;
And dying is the flame
Within my lamp.

TO THE DANCING GIRL ON NORTH LAKE

To-day,
I loiter on the lake,
And to and fro
I go
In my light craft.
The willow boughs are soft ;

A light is on the waves,
Which dazzles me.
So Spring will come
And Spring will go,
Till heads turn white.

" You dancing girl
With lovely voice.
For me, 'tis hard to cease
From drinking wine
And I exhort you all
To fill a brimming golden cup.
In Spring, the time of flowers,
To suffer ill from wine's excess
Is most romantic too."

CHANG HSIEN
A.D. 980–1078

An official and bard, who wrote many songs, but whose standard of poetry is considered low by the Chinese. Lived to be 90. Contemporary of Liu Yung.

AT THE FEAST

A red
Embroidered cloth is spread.
The curtains are of silk,
As green as jade.
A damsel in her teens,
With knowledge to admire
The talented,
Exhorts us each
To fill our cups with wine.
Her fragrant mouth is small:
Her jet-black eyebrows long.
She softly whispers in my ear:
" My home is at the turning of the road
Where shady willows grow.
A crimson apricot
Flowers at the gate."

THE PLUMS HEAR THE MUSIC OF HER FLUTE

The clouds are light,
The willows soft,
Her tresses newly dressed.
By nature she is beautiful,
With colours true
Which none can imitate.
Her flute is placed
Across her lips.
Alone she plays
In dim moonlight ;
While day declines
And sunset fades.

Vermilion lips apart :
A freshly opened cherry bud.
The leaning one
Is at the corner of the balcony.
The night is chill.
Her silken garments thin,
Her fingers cold ;
But music penetrates
The frosty woods,
And startled plums
Fall pattering down.

YEN CHI-TAO

A.D. 1100

YEN CHI-TAO was the youngest son of Yen Shu. He was a scholar and literary man. In youth he was considered gay and frivolous. His poetry is different in style from the other Sung poets. In temperament he was trustful. He never refused to oblige any one and was thought a fool. He did not succeed in getting an official position. He only wrote poetry and impoverished his family.

LET THE HARP SPEAK

Raindrops
Bid farewell to clouds and fall.
Flowing streams return not to their springs.
Sorrow that remains, when will it cease?
Bitter as the kernel of a lotus seed
Is my heart.

Curbing tears, I cannot sing.
Let the harp strings
Speak for me.
Sing the wish to meet again!
Can it be?

LIU YUNG

A.D. 1034

Liu Yung is known throughout China as a bard of the people. The musicians of his time came to him for verses to put to their tunes. It is said in China that wherever there are wells of water there you hear Liu Yung's poetry sung.

THE BUTTERFLY LOVES THE FLOWERS

In solitude
I lean
Against the ruined tower.
Soft breezes blow.
But hope has reached its end
In parting grief.
The border of the sky
Begets dark night.
The glow of hills:
The hue of grass
Have intermingled in the dusk.
My thoughts to none are known
As here I rest
Against the balustrade.

Shall I then madly drink,
And sing before the wine ?
The boundary of bliss
Is joyless still.
My girdle grows
Too spacious as my form
Diminishes.
Until the end
My love will never change.
For you
I pine.

I DAILY LOOK FOR YOU

The rain is past,
The air is crisp.
Erect beside
The River Tower,
I stand and gaze
At distant shining lakes,
And tiers and tiers
Of jade-green twilight hills.
My rambling thoughts
Are far.
I see a narrow bridge
A quiet path ;
And hazy fishing villages
Where lonely smoke ascends.

Beneath the dying sun,
Against the deep
Vermilion balustrade
I lean.
I am intoxicated yet
Unquenched.
My sorrow has no end.
The evening clouds have passed.
The autumn wind
Has long been spent.
A thousand miles away
Are friends.
In vain
I daily look for you.

SSŪ-MA KUANG
A.D. 1009-1086

A FAMOUS historian of the Sung dynasty who compiled a general history of China. A great hero of all modern schoolboys of China owing to the stories told of his childhood in every school reader.

THE TRYST

When yellow gages ripen, heavy falls the rain.
All round about the rushy ponds
The frogs are seen again.
A tryst I have,
But half the night is spent
In waiting here for him,
And idly rattling chess-men, till the wick
Falls down
Upon the candle rim.

WANG AN-SHIH
A.D. 1027–1086

A HISTORIAN, statesman, and reformer. He introduced military training for all classes in his time. His tablet was placed in the Confucian temple where it remained 140 years.

SPRING NIGHT

Extinguished is the incense in the gold imperial
    urn.
Relentlessly the water clock drips out its time.
I snuff the palace wicks,
And every gust of wind
A chilling shiver sends.
This atmosphere of spring robs man of sleep,
For shadows of the flowers, cast by the moon,
Have climbed up to the balcony.

UNDER THATCHED EAVES

Beneath my eaves of thatch
I daily sweep away the moss.
In even rows,

With my own hands
I tend my plants.
A jasper stream
Encircles all my fields ;
Two hills are ranged
Before my doors
That send a gift
Of green.

LATE IN THE TOWER SITTING IDLY

On every side
Hill light
Meets water light.
I lean
Upon the rail.
The scents of ling [1]
And lotus flowers
Are wafted
Miles and miles.
Faint breeze :
Bright moon :
No one disturbs ;
But suddenly
Out from the south
A cold, cold wind
Is sent.

[1] ling = water chestnut flower.

LEI CHÊN

A Sung dynasty poet. Date uncertain.

VILLAGE EVENINGS

The pond is overgrown with weeds.
Its waters lap the brim in ripples cold.
The sun sets where the hills divide.
Astride his ox the little herd
Is going home;
And from his pipe and heart
He makes a tuneless melody.

SU SHIH

Born on the 19th of the 12th moon, A.D. 1036
Died, 28th of the 7th moon, A.D. 1101

ONE of China's greatest writers, better known under his adopted name Su Tung-p'o. He shared the fate of most of her statesmen in being banished to a distant post. His tablet was placed in the Confucian temple for 600 years.

THE WAITING STATESMAN

I go to the palace at dawn.
Dim stars and pale moon are my light.
From braziers of gold, a fairy wind wafts
The fragrance of incense abroad.
Before the celestial throne
I stand, as erect as a crane.
In radiance, the Emperor is holding his court
Like Yü Huang [1] up-held by the clouds.

[1] Yü Huang : Supreme among the Gods.

SU SHIH

WYGELIA

To Yang Kuei Fei

The east wind gently blows
Where moonlight overflows;
And fragrant mists and dew call forth
Soft perfume of wygelia.
The night is late,
And on the terrace, moonbeams dance:
But all the flowers are now asleep.
I fear
They cannot see her standing there
Alone,
With tall red candle lifted high,
Illuminating with its flame
Her painted charm.

SU CHIEH

(Thinking of his brother Su Chieh)

When comes the bright full moon?
I raise the wine cup and interrogate
The azure heavens.
What year is this
To dwellers in the Palace of the Skies?
I wish that I might, riding on the wind,
Return there now;
But this I fear:
I could not bear the cold
In that high marble tower.

SU CHIEH

I rise
And with my shadows dance.
I feel detached from earth.
The moon
Around
The Red Pavilion moves.
It stoops and peeps in at the doors,
And shines on those who cannot sleep.
The moon should have no care ;
Yet always does it seem that she is round
When friends are far apart.
But joys and sorrows, meetings, partings, all
To mortals come.
The moon has clear and cloudy nights :
She waxes and she wanes :
This never can be changed.
I would that men could live
For evermore,
And share
The moonlight, though a thousand miles
Divides.

CH'ÊNG HAO

A.D. 1032–1085

A NATIVE of Lo-Yang. An official. With his brother Ch'eng Ying he learned poetry and wrote it.

He was a Taoist and wrote many of the Tao Scriptures and books of meditation for the priests.

THE AUTUMN MONTHS

Crystal is the stream that flows
Round a headland green as jade.
Limpid waters fresh and cool
Make the autumn's light and shade.

Severed from the dusty world
Thirty miles away,
Foam-white clouds and russet leaves
Both together sway.

SPRING DAYS COME SUDDENLY

Thin clouds:
Light winds
When noon is nigh.
By flowers
And willows
I cross the stream.
The poets
Know not
My joy of heart.
With stolen leisure
I follow youth.

CH'IN KUAN

A.D. 1048–1100

A Sung poet who produced three books of poems. A contemporary of Su Shih and Wang An-shih.

During his life regarded with more favour than Su Shih.

OF FADING BLOSSOMS

Outside the gates,
In willows green
Are cawing rooks.
The air of spring
Intoxicates.
To light
The incense bowl,
She rises from her sleep;
But alabaster wrist,
So frail,
To raise
The golden brazier is too slight.
For thinner, thinner she has grown.
Of fading blossoms now
It is the time.

WITH THE DAY

The bright translucent moon
Shines in the early hours.
The lonely inn is locked and barred.
A rat peers in the lamp
And breaks my dream.
The morning frost has sent a chill
Which penetrates my quilt.
I cannot sleep.
Outside the gate
The horses neigh,
So man
Arises with the day.

FICKLE YOUTH

Thin clouds obliterate the hills.
Outlined against the sky
Is fading grass.
The horns of guards
No longer sound
From out the watch tower high.
I rein my steed
To drink a cup of wine ;
And many old romances come to me
Like clouds and mist.
Beyond the setting sun,
Like tiny specks,

Are winter crows.
Around the lonely village flows
A stream.

My heart is melting now.
Her fragrant purse detached
She gives to me:
A silken girdle rent in two.
Amidst those in the past
The name I won
Was " Fickle Youth."
When shall we meet again ?
My sleeves are dyed with parting tears,
The hour is sad.
The towering city walls
Are out of sight.
Dim lighted lamps shine through the yellow
    dusk.

HUANG T'ING-CHIEN

A.D. 1045–1105

ONE of China's greatest scholars. Distinguished for his filial piety.

SPRING

Where has Spring gone ?
None has trod that lonely road.
Whoso knows where Spring has fled,
Call him back to live with me.

Spring has left no footsteps here.
Who can tell except the oriole ?
Ask him.
His song, a hundred times retold,
Borne by wind across the rambler rose,
None can understand.

SPRING'S RETURN

When will Spring return ?
Ask the blossom of the peach and plum :
No reply !

Homing swallows light upon their nests:
Wind is blowing free:
Snow of pear:
Petals of my tree
Fly confusedly
In the Western Court.
There, above, the graceful moon appears.
Like that One—remote as Heaven.
Would that she might let her image be
Clearly seen.
And that we might always live together
Here.

DIVINING

I wish to see
But cannot see.
I wish to meet
But near I cannot be.
I test and ask
How much he loves me still.
The reed [1] reveals
It not.
Such hatefulness!

The tears I cannot stay;
But bear my grief.
Of human sorrow like to this
There is no skill to sound its depth.

[1] reed: In divination a hollow bamboo reed is used.

TOO LATE

The river's Western bank
Is fringed by misty trees.
I cannot see the road
Upon the Eastern side.
But I imagine in my dreams
That I can go there without fear
Of being hindered by the river.

Before my lamp I write
Unnumbered letters to my friends.
But I have no one to convey them.
I'll seek the lone wild-goose
And bid him go.
But autumn now is at an end
And all the geese are gone.

CHOU PANG-YEN

A.D. 1057–1121

An official of high rank. A gifted poet and musician. Known throughout China. He wrote many love songs. His lyrics are considered better than Liu Yung's.

AFTER CAROUSING

Gloomy autumn days return.
Bleaker grow the nights.
Sad and cold my court becomes.
Here I stand alone
Listening to the winter sounds.
Clouds obscure all shadows of the flying geese.

Night is deep.
Guests are gone.
On the wall and me
Shines a single lamp.
Wakened from the sleep of wine
How can I exhaust this endless night?

A WIND-TOSSED CLOUD

Tao Chi Streamlet flows unchecked:
Lotus roots, in autumn cleft,
Never join as one again.
On a time I waited there
By the arched vermilion bridge.
Now I trace where yellow leaves
Strew the ground, and walk alone.

In the mist a row of peaks:
Azure hills innumerable.
Where the wild goose spreads its wings,
Sunset burns and fades.
Man is like a wind-tossed cloud
Fallen in the river's surge.
All my heart's emotions seem
Willow seed rain-battered to the ground.

I WRITE TO HER

Beneath the leafy trees,
The setting sun
Is shining on the lake.
The tiny ripples curl
And sink, and sink,
A thousand miles.
Upon the bridge
The bitter wind
Blows stingingly.

I stand awhile,
At yellow dusk,
To watch the lantern fair.

Outside my old
Low eaved abode,
I hear catalpa leaves
Fall fluttering down.
Relinquishing
My lonely quilt,
I rise repeatedly ;
But who is there to know
I write to her.

SHE SINGS THE SONG OF GOLDEN THREADS

Before the tower, an aged tree.
Beyond the willow, endless, endless roads
That meet the jade
Suspended corners of the sky.
The lofty crenellated city walls
Disclose a row of peaks.
My travel-wearied eyes
Are kindled by the sight
Of hills like these.
In wordless grief
Alone I stand,
While dusky rooks
In pairs and pairs fly home.

THE SONG OF GOLDEN THREADS

In Peace and Pleasure Lane
Romances pass like showers.
Returning after many years,
All weary of pursuing wine shop flags
And drums of theatres,
To-night
How fortunate I am;
For one,
As lovely as a fairy of the moon,
Now raises up her sunset sleeves
To fill a cup of wine for me,
And sing the Song of Golden Threads.

LI C'HING-CHAO
A.D. 1081–1140

THE most distinguished woman scholar of China. Her father Li Ke-fei was a lifelong friend of Su Shih.

THE WIDOW

Seek, seek: search, search:
Cold, cold: bare, bare:
Grief: grief. Cruel, cruel grief.
Now warm, then like the autumn, cold again.
How hard to calm the heart!
With tiny cups of lightest wine,
How can the cold, sent by the sharp night wind,
Be overcome?

The wild-geese flying pass,
That set the heart to ache,
Like pensive memories
Of friends of old and times gone by.

Beside my window, here, I pause alone.
When will the night descend?
Chrysanthemums bestrew the ground
In withered heaps.

Which can be plucked?
Catalpa leaves are rustling with the misty rain:
And rain-drops patter in the yellow dusk;
And sorrow, sorrow, sorrowing;
Can such a word as this
Be ever ended?

THE WIDOW

The wind has ceased.
The earth is sweet.
The flowers fade.
The day is done.
In weariness
I still neglect
To dress my hair.
His things are here
Though he has gone.
All, all is past.
No word is said;
And yet my tears fall.

I hear that spring is glorious still
At River Shuang.
I, too, would sail there in a little boat.
Ah, but I fear
On River Shuang
The boats are frail,
They cannot bear
My weight of care.

HSIANG HAO

Date unknown

A BARD of the people who wrote lyrics in the language of the people. A native of Ho Nan province. There is no authentic history of him.

AT EARLY DAWN

A river wide,
I cross
At early dawn ;
And as I glide,
I see the white hoar-frost
And pale cold moon.
A solitary broken bridge
Displays a branch
Of flowering plum
Athwart its southern end,
Like her in slender grace,
Of pearl-white hue.
At this, I turn my thoughts to her again.
Ah ! these disturbing thoughts !
When will they cease ?

CHU TUN-JU

A.D. 1080–?

A NATIVE of Ho Nan province. Famous as a poet when he was young. He was called by the Emperor to serve as a high official but declined. When asked a second time he consented, but lost his position later because of slanderous accusations by his enemies. He lived to a great age. His poetry is divided into three kinds. In youth he wrote joyful poetry; in middle age sorrowful, when the Sung dynasty became decadent. Finally in old age his poems reveal a mellow philosophy.

THE PEERLESS LADY

The rain
Of spring
Like dust
Descends.
The yellow willow leaves
Are wet.
The wind has blown
Aslant
The broidered screen.
Revealing, all without
The window, cold and green.

CHU TUN-JU

> The peerless lady trims
> The altar lamps.
> She dries her tears
> While leaning on her harp.
> At Tzŭ Ku's [1] shrine
> The incense burns.
> To ask for news
> From East of Liao.

THE FISHERMAN

He turns his head and leaves the world,
Is sober or bemused with wine at will.
A living earned with creel and coat of reeds,
Or clad in frost, to face the driving snow.

When winds are calm, at eve,
His rod and hook are still.
The new moon shines above;
And in the waters of the mere
It shines below.
A thousand miles of sky
And water are one hue.
He watches there a swan appear
And disappear.

The fisherman, since he was born,
Has only boon companions in his rod and line.
He turns his boat

[1] Tzŭ Ku = Purple Goddess.

THE FISHERMAN

And rows it to and fro:
Like flying in the air
He leaves no trace.

The water-rushes flower and fade.
Permit them then to live their fleeting life.
To quaff his yellow wine
And sleep, his policy.
The wind and rain last night
Spread over all the river's face.
The fisher never heard the storm.

His tiny boat with stunted oar, he plies.
The mist at twilight cages up
The jade-hued night.
The Northern geese and sea-gulls come
To parting of the ways,
And mingle with the river and the skies.
A basket-full of pearly scales
And warm vibrating fins,
The fisherman exchanges for his wine.
A following wind:
A single sail:
With these
Now who can urge him rest awhile?

He suddenly arrives.
He fishes here and there,
As though he knew
The whereabouts of shoals
And saw their sign;

For nature places in his hand
A rod and line,
These thousand leagues of water
To subdue.

The dusty world,
Its past and present vanish as the turning of his
    boat,
As swiftly as the sea-gull and the heron which
    have flown.
The fisherman is free
From every bondage of the world.
He goes from North to South,
From East to West, at will.

BY THE BROOK

A branch of peach
Blooms by the brook.
No garden wall
Imprisons it.
And far away
Within the valley deep,
It seems to hide itself
With Spring.

"My secret thoughts,
Who knows them all?
And who can pluck me for a poet's theme?
The moon has come to seek me here
In fragrance and romance
Alone."

CHU HSI
A.D. 1130-1200

THE most voluminous of Chinese writers whose interpretations of the Confucian books are the only authorized ones.

PARABLE OF LEARNING TRUTH

Last night, the Spring tide rose in flood,
The battlemented ship
That, stranded yesterday,
Defied the strength of man to launch,
Now, like a feather light,
With easy buoyancy
Glides down mid-stream.

POMEGRANATE FLOWERS IN SPRING

Pomegranate flowers
Of May
Are dazzling bright ;
Among the branches fruit is hid.
How sad it is
That chariots
And horses are not here
To bring spectators for the topsy-turvy moss :
And scarlet fallen bloom.

HSIN CH'I-CHI

A.D. 1140–1207

A WARRIOR of great valour who produced many books of poetry.

ON THE ROAD

The jackdaw, from its branch,
Is startled by the moon's bright light.
A gentle breeze, at midnight, wakes
Cicadas into tune.
And everywhere
Among the fragrant flowering rice,
The croaking of the frogs
Proclaim abundant harvesting.
And gleaming in the outer sky
Are seven or eight dim stars;
Before the hills
Fall one or two
Light drops of rain.
I pass the old thatched inn,
Beside the forest's rim,

And reach the turning of the road,
Where I espy
A little bridge
Across a stream.

LIFE

Ten thousand dim activities
Have swiftly passed :
A hundred years
Like rushes early sered
Or willows withered and decayed.
And now in life,
Of value, what is left to do ?
To drink :
To roam :
To sleep :

To pay one's tax
Before it is demanded :
To estimate
One's income and expenditure !
Your old men still control
A few affairs.
Bamboos,
The hills,
The streams.

SORROW'S TASTE

When I was young,
Naught of sorrow's taste
I knew.
I loved to climb the storied tower.
I loved to climb the storied tower,
Of sorrow speak,
To write new odes.

Now I am old,
All of sorrow's taste
I know.
I wish to speak, but I refrain.
I wish to speak, but I refrain,
And merely say,
"The autumn's fresh and cool."

ON THE ROAD TO PO-SHAN

Low eaves and thatch,
Of green, green river grass.
There warmed with wine,
In Southern accents, happily,
The white-haired couple chat.

The oldest son
Is raking beans
Upon the river's Eastern bank.

The second son
Is weaving chicken coops.
But idle is the youngest son;
For at the river's head,
He watches others split
Brown lotus seeds.

MY NEW HOUSE ON LAKE TAI

The garden on Lake Tai
Is near completion now.
The cranes complain,
The wild apes are disturbed,
Yet Chia Hsien has not come.
My thoughts are like
The misty clouds
Above the hills.
These robes of state
Seem like the dust.
When purpose flags
One should be early freed
To travel home.
Not for the soup of herbs
Alone,
Nor dish of perch.

Upon the autumn river yonder gaze,
And watch the startled geese
Escaping from the hunter's darts.
Behold the boats
Returning from the frightening waves!

Upon the hill crest's Eastern slope
Another hut of grasses thatch for me,
With doors and windows opening on the lake,
Along the banks
Young willows should be planted first,
For fishing from a boat;
And sparsely hedge the bamboo grove,
But hinder not the view
Of flowering plum.
Chrysanthemums of autumn made for feasting
And Spring-time's orchid, for adornment,
Are left for me to plant
With my own hand.
I meditate on these
A long, long while.
I fear
The Emperor
Will never spare me.
This thought arrests me now.
Irresolute I am.

MIDNIGHT AMONG THE HILLS

My Life's affairs decrease.
My autumn thoughts
Are clear
Unto the depths.
'Tis midnight, yet
My pillow still records
Faint sounds.

I HEAR THE MONASTERY BELL

Why do the little brooks not cease?
Why are they not at rest?
The moon has reached
That sad pale gold
Of early dawn.
The cock's dim crow
Is heard afar;
Among the hills,
There are no things
Called wealth and fame.
Then why are people walking in the hills
Before the daylight comes?

AT MIDNIGHT I HEAR THE MONASTERY BELL

My life is in the midst of wine cups told,
And everything is void.
In olden days
Some three or five
Brave heroes lived.
The rain beat down.
The wind blew cold.
Now where are all the Halls
Of Ch'in and Han?

I dreamed that I returned
To circles of my youth,
To dance and sing awhile.
Mistakenly the aged priest
Has struck the temple bell.

It rouses me.
I cannot sleep.
The West wind curls
About the earth.

SHE IS GONE

When the swallows returned last year,
In the broidery room they built a nest,
From the path by the flowers they gathered clay,
Over harp and books they scattered the dust.

When the swallows returned this year,
No one heard their twittering words;
For the one who rolled up the screen of the door,
Is no longer seen.
In the amber twilight there falls
A shower of pattering rain.

THE TUNE OF THE STREAM

With my shadow I walk
By the rivulet.
In the limpid stream the sky is held;
In the sky are moving clouds;
And I seem to walk with the moving clouds.

Then I lustily carol, who answers me?
In the empty valley there rises a sound.
Not the voice of a spirit or fairy fay,
But the tune of the stream
Where the fallen petals of peach
Are swiftly carried away.

YEH SHIH
A.D. 1150–1223

An official under the Sung Emperor of his time. He was banished from the court because of slanderous accusations which brought about his disgrace. He then became a poet.

THE LITTLE GARDEN

Reluctantly I crush, with rough shod feet,
The soft green moss,
To rap ten times upon the wooden gate ;
But still it opens not.
The garden, all ablaze with Spring,
Is closed in vain.
For, there, a crimson spray
Of apricot
Beyond the wall escapes.

LU YU

A.D. 1125–1201

THE greatest poet of the Southern Sungs. Wrote poetry at the age of 12. In youth a valorous warrior, in old age he lost all worldly ambition and only interested himself in nature.

THE WARRIORS

Since the autumn came
To the borders in the North,
Sky and earth have changed.
Hêng Yang geese have no intent to stay;
South they swiftly fly.
Mountains range a thousandfold.
Everywhere
Echoes rise of warriors' horns.
Wisps of mist : a setting sun :
There a lonely city stands,
With its portals closed.

Muddy wine, a cup, ten thousand miles from home.
Unsubdued the Northern tribes remain.
Not a warrior may return.

EVERYTHING WILL CHANGE

Frost has covered all the ground.
Softly floats the music of their flutes ;
White-haired generals,
Weeping warriors
Cannot sleep.

THE AGED WARRIOR

Ten thousand miles
I travelled, in the past,
To seek distinction : military fame.
I guarded Liang Chou all alone
Astride my horse.
Of frontiers,
Of boundaries,
Where are those faded dreams ?
Where vanished now ?
My sable robe is darkened by the dust.
The Mongols are unconquered still.
My hair has reached its autumn time.
My tears unheeded fall.
Who understands this life ?
My heart is still in Turkestan—
My being in the South.

TO-MORROW EVERYTHING WILL CHANGE. THE
RAIN WILL SCATTER THE PEACH BLOOM

A decade of travelling,
Of singing
And buying wine,

And yet
You came not to Ching Hua.
Why come you unheralded now,
And only
To leave me so soon?
Ah, here at the Rest House
Are mist and long grasses.
Your snowy white hairs are to face
The wind and the sand.

The edge of the world
I see from this height.
Outside the pavilion
Are ten thousand houses,
And rain softly falling.
To-morrow I fear
The peach bloom and you will be gone.

THE PILGRIM THINKS AND DREAMS

The pilgrim thinks sadly
Of home.
His sorrow like silk
From cocoons
A thousand yards long.
He dreams of the lake.
Where the misty rain falls.
And he sees innumerable hills :
He thinks of his parents

LATE IN THE YEAR

Who pardon
The follies of youth :
The signs of the Spring :
The fall of the flowers :
The swallows that fly
Again to the eaves.
He sighs at the passing
Of time.

LATE IN THE YEAR

O late in the year,
I love to return to the East.
I brush from my robes
The dust of the town.
I choose me a place
Begirt by the tumbling hills ;
And fish from a pool
Both sapphire and clear.

I barter my fish.
With wine I am dazed
Yet sober withal.
The thoughts of my heart
I give to my flute.
My home is afar
Beyond the white tiers
Of ten thousand clouds.
I know all the sea-gulls
That fly in between.

THE MELANCHOLY VOICE OF THE OWL

Under the thatched
Roof, it is silent,
From the small river
Rises a storm.
Evening descends.
Late is the spring.
Mute is the oriole
Deep in the woods.
Hushed is the sparrow
Wrapped in its nest.
Only the owl hoots,
All else is still.

Stirred by its calling,
Urged into tears,
Dreams are all shattered.
Choosing the densest
Trees in the coppice,
There it alights.
Even amidst
Hills of my home,
Sad is the owl's voice.
Now having roamed
Half of a lifetime,
What are my feelings
Hearing its cries ?

CHIANG K'UEI

A.D. 1155-1235

A CIVIL official, and a native of Hu Pei province. His poetry is slow and sedate. His poems are considered by the Chinese as superior to his lyrics.

WHITE PLUM BLOSSOMS

Snowflakes frail
Scatter in the park,
By the Southern stream.
In the mansion old,
Cold, bleak Spring has locked
Host and guests.
Snowy plum trees in the garden stand,
Each complaining of the East wind's tardiness.
Blossoms on their tips have not yet burst,
Yet their hidden fragrance is dispersed.

Bring the guests.
Plum trees here will call a feast :
Drink your health.
Long live flowers !

Crush the petals for the wine.
Cut the snow and carve new rhymes.
Pace the garden round, a thousand times.

THE LANTERN FESTIVAL

1. *I look upon the Lanterns*

The festive time has come
To every one, in every place.
Before the curtained chariot
Appears,
The horses neigh
The grey-haired scholar has no mounted guards.
His little daughter, only, follows him
Astride the shoulder of a serving-man.

The fair is full of flowers.
Chill moon-light penetrates my robe.
Romances of my youth
Bring sorrow in old age.
The cold of Spring is slight
On Sandy River Pool
To-night.
I watch the pleasure seekers one by one
Return.

THE LANTERN FESTIVAL

2. *This Evening I do not Venture Out*

Remember yesterday!
The preparation for the festival:
The willows scant,
The tiny blossoms of the plum.
To-night is just the time for gaiety.
I fear the cold of Spring
And close my wooden door.
Its curtain hangs before it silently.
The moon appears to sympathize with me.
My past emotions only are revealed
In lyrics old.
At midnight, dark mimosa shadows fall.
The neighbour's daughters pass.
I hear them laugh
And chatter as they homeward wend.

3. *The Dream*

Unceasingly the River Fei
Flows East.
The seeds of love
I never should have sown.
I see you dimmer in my dreams
Than painted on a scroll.
Ah! suddenly
The cries of mountain birds,
From out the darkness, waken me.

Before the green of Spring
Already is my hair like whitened silk.
Long years of parting dull the sorrow of the heart.
Who knows if yearly, at the Scarlet Lantern Feast
We each shall meditate alone ?

4. *The Lanterns*

Along the Road
On either side
A thousand silver candles reel and dance.
Continuously, the East wind blows
Below the Red Pavilion's eaves.
Who recognizes Tu Po Tzŭ's
Thrice transmigrated soul ?
To-morrow, Spring will pass
Across the peach tree twigs.
Then gradually the sound of drums
Will fade away.
The pleasure seekers all
Will scatter home.
And melancholy will descend
On me again.
The moon alone will comprehend.

LIU K'Ê-CHUANG

A.D. 1187-1269

A NATIVE of Fu Chien province and an official. Born of a noble official family. Some of his poems offended the Emperor so he lost his official post. He became feeble and diseased in body and finally lost the sight of both eyes. He died at 38.

Liu K'ê-Chuang wrote nearly 200 books of poetry. A great many of his poems are lost.

TO A DANCING GIRL

Slender waist
Girdled by white silk,
Light and frail.
With a single hand
Might she be
Carried far.
Build a high pavilion tower,
From the wind protect her there.
Do not let the startled swan
Fly away.

Fragrant jade-white face.
Soft and warm,

Smiling,
Frowning :
Equal charm.
Now her eyebrows speak,
Craving answers from the youth :
Knowing not that she had danced the I. Chou [1]
Wrong.

A DREAM

Where shall I meet you ?
Climb up Precious Hair Pin Tower ?
Visit Brazen Bird Pavilion ?
Call the cook to slice the whale's meat
From the Eastern Sea.
Call the keeper of the house
On the Western Border
To exhibit
Dragon Child's abode.
You and T'sao
Are the only heroes
In the world.
All the rest are not
Fit to drink with us.
In a thousand chariots
Men of genius,
Skilful swordsmen,
Come from South of Yen,
Come from North of Chao.

[1] I. Chou = name of Chinese dance.

FLOWERS

Drink
Deeply.
Painted drums, like thunder, roll,
By the early cock I'm summoned back.
Years have passed,
Nothing is achieved.
Old the scholar grows.
Opportunity arrives too late.
If
General Li had met the High Imperial One,
Titles and ten thousand houses
Then were easily won.
I arise and robe myself.
Melancholy recollections come.
Valour gives
Birth to grief.

FLOWERS

Flake on flake
Of butterfly
Filmy robes.
Fleck on fleck
Of tiny scarlet specks.
If Heaven tends not the flowers,
Their hundred kinds
A thousand skilful arts
Possess.

The dawn reveals
The tree-tops thick with bloom;
But few are left at night
Upon the branches' tips.
If Heaven does tend the flowers,
Why are they scattered by the rain,
And fanned by wind away?

THE ORIOLE SHUTTLE

A golden oriole, threading in and out of willow bloom,
With chatter, chatter, chatter like a weaver's loom.
In Spring, the flowers resemble gilded gay brocade.
When will this happy bird have all its fabric made?

CHIANG CHIEH
A.D. 1250-1310

A NATIVE of Chê Chiang province during the reign of the last of the Sung Emperors. Under the Yüan dynasty he was called by the Emperor to a high official post but he resolutely refused to take office. He continued to live among the hills, writing poetry.

TIME IS LEAVING US BEHIND

Springtime melancholy
Needs the pouring out of wine.
Boats are on the river
Rocking;
Wine shop signs
Beckon me.
Chiu Niang Ford!
Tai Niang Bridge!
Where the wind blows!
Where the rain falls.
When shall I be
Homeward going?
There to cleanse my travelling robes:
Light the heart-shaped incense:

Play the silver *sheng* [1]
Time is fleeting:
Leaving us behind.
Cherries there have reddened:
Plantain leaves turned green.

AUTUMN SOUNDS

Gold chrysanthemums
In the shadowy lane.
Russet leaves by windows low.
Bean-rain [2] sounds
Carried by the wind,
Make sad autumn tunes.
Five-and-twenty beats
From the watch-tower steal:
Nor can sound of bronzed bell be locked inside.
Far away is he.
Whence the sound of tinkling jade?
Music of the tiny bells
Underneath the eaves.

Horns are sounding
With the setting moon
Gradually, among the tents,
Horses move.
Sounds of pipes arise from every side.

[1] *Sheng* = a Chinese musical instrument.
[2] Bean-rain = the first heavy rain of Spring which saturates the soya beans.

WHO COMES TO GATHER FLOWERS?

Brightly twinkle neighbours' lights,
There the washing-clapper sounds
Still are heard.
Crickets chirp their grief until the dawn:
Then their sad unfinished tale is shared
By the melancholy voices of wild-geese.

WHO COMES TO GATHER FLOWERS?

A shadow on the window screen!
Who comes to gather flowers?
Now let her pluck them if she will.
Who knows where she will take them?

Beneath the eaves
The sprays are best.
Pluck longer these;
And you who gather flowers
Remember, please,
To wear them in your hair.

MISCELLANEOUS LYRICS AND SONGS

Collected by DR. T. Z. KOO
Translated by C. M. CANDLIN
(SEE *Songs of Cathay*)

LOVE'S LAMENT IN MID-AUTUMN

Author unknown.

Light winds toss
Cinnamon perfume,
Under chilly Autumn's
Pale round moon,
Who is gaily warbling as a Phœnix calls her mate?
Music lures me from my West room;
Now I cross the stream.
Covet not the wild flowers' fragrance!
Thinking of my absent one, my scarlet gown is wet with tears.

PAN CH'IAO'S PHILOSOPHY

By CHENG PAN CH'IAO, a famous scholar, painter, and poet of great talent of the Ch'ing dynasty, during the reign of Ch'ien Lung.

Old fisherman
With your fishing rod,
Near to the cliff
In the bay!
Your boat goes to and fro.
Care-free are you.
Sea-gulls fly like specks;
Wavelets sparkle far,
Soft reeds rustle,
And cold grows the day.
High he lilts a ditty,
While slants the sun.
A moment then—
Shadows ripple gold.
"Lift up your head,
The moon is on the hill."

Old scholar wise
In your white room,
Teaching Tang Yu
And customs old!
Your pupils have attained
To high degrees.
Vassals throng their gates.

Tigers fierce are they.
In the streets their banners wave ;
As dragons they move.
At dawn their glories fade,
Like a spring dream.
Naught can compare
With a grass-grown gate,
In a by-lane,
And teaching scholars young.

MY BEAUTIFUL ONE

By LIU CHI, 1311-1375. A poet of the Yüan dynasty.

Rain is in the air ;
Wind arises now ;
Fitfully the grass
Bends before the breeze.
Cassia flowers bow ;
Ruffled petals fall ;
Tender leaves are shed ;
Whirls of dust dance in the sky.
Quivering curtains flap ;
Silken draperies
Sway upon my door ;
Loneliness descends
As I dream of thee ;
Limitless blue sky,
Hill and sea,
Sever you and me.

Aimlessly, the birds
Fly among the clouds;
Greetings I would send,
On their pinions fleet.
Rivers flowing East
Never do return;
Fragrant orchids bloom
Only for a day;
Silent is her harp;
Idle lies her flute.
As I gazed last night
At the gleaming moon;
Crooning restlessly,
Lonely was my soul.
Will each morn
Always be like this?

SPRING TIDINGS

Author unknown.

Spring tidings everywhere,
Revealed in every face.
Mimosa flowers their shadows cast.
My dreams are butterflies.
The quince intoxicates.
A gulf divides us:
I pluck the willow—
For me
No fairy bridge of birds.

Before a silver lamp, alone, I weep ;
Grow frail as Hsiao Man.[1]
The bloom of youth is past.
When shall we share a night like this,
A night like this,
And meet beneath the bright full moon ?

THOUGHTS OF LOVE

A famous folk-song. Several versions are in existence, but the author is unknown.

In sunny days of Spring
Thoughts come and go.
A hundred kinds of grass
Sprout up and grow.
The misty willows bend.
And he has gone : a pilgrim far away.
My mirror's gauzy screen I draw aside ;
Ah, pity me ; adorned for none to see.
I wonder has he, there, another fairy bride ?
Does he forget our former happy days ?
My heaven !
And such a gallant, gallant youth,
How can your heart then change ?
And you were such a gallant youth,
How can your heart then change ?

[1] Hsiao Man = a noted Chinese beauty, famous for her slenderness.

The water lilies float ;
Thoughts come and go.
My raven locks unbound
Blow to and fro.
The summer heat returns ;
And you have gone ; Oh, whither fare you now ?
The tears like Hsiang Lake fall upon my breast.
Ah, pity me ; alone I look for you.
And sit in my pavilion with embroidery.
When shall we meet and dwell on parted days ?
My heaven !
To sever faithful loving ones
How could you have the heart ?
To sever from a loving wife
How could you have the heart ?

With fragrant cinnamon
Thoughts come and go.
The autumn insects chirp :
Chirp shrill and low.
My heart is vexed in me.
Remote are you, and mountain peaks divide.
Now who is playing on a flute of jade ?
So desolate : I fear its mournful strain ;
For high above I hear the lone swan's piercing
    cry ;
Ah, who will take a letter full of love ?
My heaven !
And do you know I sit alone
At home and long for you ?

And do you know I sit alone
At home and long for you?

In Winter, blooms the plum:
Thoughts come and go.
And on the earth like down,
Fall flakes of snow.
The cold is hard to bear.
You're far away, and never have returned.
I ponder, "Are you cold?" and foolishly
" At night, who spreads your mat and folds your
    quilt?"
Do you forget ungratefully, my kindness now?
So young you are and I'm a woman weak.
My universe!
And if you should unfaithful prove,
Above your head is Heaven.
And if you should unfaithful prove,
Above your head is Heaven.

The seasons of the year
Pass, sad and slow.
Without the gate a knock—
His voice I know!
So joyfully I go;
With timid, fearful steps the portal reach,
I place my hands upon his shoulders now.
'Tis dawn, I see his precious face again—
Together, then we enter these ancestral halls,
To cleanse our hearts and sacrifice to Heaven.

My universe !
A day of perfect happiness :
The end of anxious thoughts.
A day of perfect happiness :
The end of anxious thoughts.

MÊNG CHIANG NÜ'S LAMENT

Author unknown.

The story is based upon a legend connected with the building of the Great Wall. Mêng Chiang Nü's husband, Wan Chi-liang, was impressed into a labour gang and sent North to build the Great Wall. As no word came from him, she became alarmed and set out alone to find him.

Plum flowers at New Year bring new Spring.
Red lamps are lit at every door.
Each family is united then.
But he has gone to build the Wall.

The second month brings apricots.
The swifts alight on Southern walls.
Their nests are moulded trim and neat
They poise in pairs on painted beams.

March heralds Ching Ming, peaches bloom.
The peach is red, the willow green.
White paper burns on every grave.
His grave is lonely chill and bare.

Silk-worms and ramblers April brings.
The leaves of mulberry trees we pull.
We hang our baskets on the twigs.
I pull a handful as I weep.

Pomegranates ripen in the rains
Of May, and yellow gages fall.
In every field are tender plants.
My fields are full of weeds, in heaps.

June lotus lilies bring great heat;
Insects that sting fly everywhere.
My flesh is pierced, my blood is drawn.
Leave Wan Chi-liang's alone untouched.

Balsams in July; Autumn's near.
Our Winter clothes are made anew
Some red, some black, some green or blue.
My boxes, all are still unfilled.

In August, Cassia flowers bloom.
On lone swan's wings the letters come.
The gossips gossip all the day.
His garments none will ever bring.

September brings chrysanthemums.
New wine is drunk, and heat returns.
I shun the brimming bowl of wine,
For I shall never drink alone.

Hibiscus in October comes.
The rice is milled, the tax is paid.
Each home has stones to grind the meal;
My threshing floor at home is bare.

Snow flakes and ice November brings.
I take his clothes a thousand miles.
The ravens lead me, step by step.
I weep until I reach the Wall.

Plum flowers to end the busy year.
Each home kills fatted pigs and sheep.
The New Year comes with noisy cheer.
I weep uncomforted alone.

SONG OF "CH'ING MING"

Author unknown.

Famous Chinese folk-song.

After fallen rain
From my home I go.
Willow springs now grow
Ch'ing Ming's [1] here again
By the East gate
Limpid streams flow :

[1] Ch'ing Ming = a Spring rite when the ancestral graves are visited, white paper money is placed on them, and incense is burned.

CH'ING MING

Bright the hills glow. Ah!
Scenes to sadden me.
Ah! . . .
Scenes to sadden me.

Willow bending there;
Orioles sing to me.
Broidered shoes I wear,
Sewed in secrecy;
Walk the maidens,
All around me,
Neat and pretty. Ah!
Flowers their fragrance waft.
Ah! . . .
Flowers their fragrance waft.

Few the moons of life;
Tangled mounds of grass.
In a dawn; with strife,
All the brave ones pass
Through the tombs' gate,
Where with clatter
Grey ghosts chatter. Ah!
Who can know my grief?
Ah! . . .
Who can know my grief?

TSAO CHÜN GOES TO MONGOLIA

Author unknown.

During the latter part of the Han dynasty, China was often harassed by marauding bands of Mongols. In order to secure relief for his kingdom from these invasions, the Emperor entered into a peace pact with them. One condition in this pact was that the Mongol chieftain should wed as his wife one of the women of the Imperial household. Wang Tsao Chün, a most talented and beautiful lady, was selected for this unwelcome honour and commanded to go to Mongolia. In this song, she is lamenting her fate as she bids farewell to the Imperial Court.

In Wei Yang Palace lived I year by year.
    Ah!
Spring days were late, autumn nights were long.
My Prince was kind; cruel is fate.
By command I go.
    Ah!
Bitter is my woe.

I ride, lamenting, holding my guitar.
    Ah!
Gold clouds of sand shadow the Great Wall.
The sky grows dark; veiled are the stars.
Mongol horns are sad.
    Ah!
Mournful is their sound.

TO MONGOLIA

The tears from my two eyes stream down and fall.
>Ah!

Who sees my grief, leaving gates of Han?
My Dragon Prince! My Phœnix Court!
Hills of Yen, farewell!
>Ah!

Sorrowful, I go.